C000255566

Contents

Your daughter's engaged 8

Counting the cost 18

A dad, not just a wallet 32

Family matters 40

Up-to-date dads 54

What to wear 64

The big day 80

Pray silence… 96

About Confetti.co.uk 128

THE FATHER OF THE BRIDE'S WEDDING

So, your little girl is getting married, and you're the proud father of the bride. What do you need to do to make sure that life from now until The Big Day runs as smoothly as possible?

The Father of the Bride's Wedding

The guide to your role

from **confetti.co.uk**
don't get married without us…

First published in 2004 by Octopus Publishing Group,
2–4 Heron Quays, London E14 4JP
www.conran-octopus.co.uk

A catalogue record for this book is available
from the British Library.
ISBN 1 84091 364 9

Publishing Director Lorraine Dickey
Senior Editor Katey Day
Assistant Editor Sybella Marlow
Art Director Chi Lam
Designer Jeremy Tilston
Assistant Production Controller Natalie Moore

INTRODUCTION

Traditionally, the only requirement of the
father of the bride was that he should
have deep pockets. Today, the modern
father of the bride needs to have the
diplomatic skills of a UN ambassador,
the lightning reactions of a Wimbledon
tennis player and the philosophic
capabilities of Socrates.

Yes, just when you thought it was as simple as knowing your traditional responsibilities, your daughter is going to want to do it her way. Hasn't she always?

INTRODUCTION

This book is designed to guide you through the highs and lows, fun and furore and ins and outs of being a modern day father of the bride, from the engagement to the moment you finish your speech, visiting all points in between.

Your daughter's
engaged

Getting the news

Your prospective son-in-law may give you prior warning by asking for your permission to seek your daughter's hand in marriage (see page 14). If not, happy couples have been known to announce the news to proud parents by phone, in person, via email, at parties and even over the tannoy at the airport.

Announcing the news

After this, it's usually down to you to make the official announcement to the rest of the world, often via an insert in a local or national newspaper.

Announcing the engagement

In local papers, the announcement is placed in the 'Notices' section, and the standard format is as follows:

Mr and Mrs Trevor Jones of Midsummer Cottage, Norton, are delighted to announce the engagement of their daughter Felicity Jane to Mark Edward, son of Mr and Mrs Anthony Shaw of Kingsbridge, Devon.

How to announce the news

In national newspapers, the announcement
is placed in the Court and Social section,
and the standard format is as follows:

Mr J.D. Roe, Miss I.A. Winter

The engagement is announced between

Jeremy David, eldest son of Mr and Mrs

Thomas Roe of Southsea, Hants,

and Isobel Ann Winter,

middle daughter of Mr and Mrs Rory Winter

of Salterton, Wiltshire.

The announcement may also be made on

www.confetti.co.uk

Gaining a son...

It is traditional for the groom's parents to 'call on' the bride's parents soon after their children have decided to marry, but it doesn't always happen nowadays. Generally, the parents will meet at some stage during the engagement, but these days engagements are longer and there doesn't seem to be any hurry to make the introductions. It's a nice idea, though, to arrange a get-together as soon after the engagement announcement as possible.

Maintaining tradition

In a recent poll, 65 per cent answered 'yes' to the question, 'Should potential grooms ask permission from the bride's father?' It seems that seeking the permission of the father (or mother, or both) is alive and well, and may be coming to a house near you soon!

If he asks for permission

With many engagements taking place during romantic holidays abroad, he may ask for permission on the phone. Whether he's in the room or on the end of a long-distance line, keep it light, don't rib him too much and remember, it's probably taken a lot of guts for him to do this!

If he doesn't ask…

As more and more couples live together before marriage, and fewer brides are married from home, traditions such as asking permission to marry may no longer be appropriate, so don't feel offended if he doesn't ask first.

Don't be offended

He may well be doing this out of respect
for your daughter. If he knows her well
enough to marry her, he might also know
that she has an independent streak a mile
wide and would baulk at the thought
of someone asking her father for her
hand in marriage. Or maybe she
proposed to him!

Counting the cost

COUNTING THE COST

As the father of the bride, your role is to
support your daughter in every way.
Usually, this also means financially!
So what's new?

Some fathers choose to participate in all
aspects of the wedding preparations; others
prefer to stand back and allow the groom,
bride and her mother make the
arrangements. Either way is fine.

The traditional expense

Traditionally, the bride's family pays for:

Engagement and wedding press
announcements

The dresses

Outfits for the mother and
father of the bride

Flowers for the church and reception

Photographer

Most of the transport

Wedding stationery

The big one: the reception and
all its trimmings

How much?

Nowadays, the cost of even the most modest wedding can be astronomical. In fact, the average wedding costs £15,000!

A wise father will set his budget as early as possible and advise the couple how much he is able and willing to spend. Then there can be no misunderstandings and the couple are able to budget accordingly.

The price of love

These are average costs compiled from the budgets of Confetti users.

Wedding cake – £200
Catering, food and drink – £3000
Bride's dress – £700
Bridesmaids' dresses and accessories – £150 (per head)
Entertainment – £300
Venue hire – £2500

Help at hand

For more information on average costs and for a free budget planner to keep tabs on the expense, visit: www.confetti.co.uk/weddings/planning _tools/default.asp

Sharing the load

Some tasks in the preparation for the big day traditionally belong to you, but any or all of these may instead be undertaken either by the bridal couple or by other members of the bride's family or close friends. And frankly, your daughter may well have decided already what she wants you to do!

Going halves

The two sets of parents may wish to share the cost of the wedding between them. In this case, it's best to make sure you have a good working relationship between you, rather than trying to coordinate everything via the bride and groom.

Contributions

Some parents like to give a sum of money to be spent as the happy couple wishes; others prefer to contribute specific items. If you choose the second option, make sure you confer with your daughter – you don't want to surprise her with a seven-tier, pink-iced confection of a wedding cake if she's chosen a burgundy-and-gold colour scheme.

Contributions

Sensible fathers realize that paying for a part or a whole of their daughter's wedding means just that — it's her wedding. If you want a comfortable life, don't try to influence her choices unless she asks for help or advice.

Guest who's coming to dinner

In the past, the bride's parents paid for and hosted the wedding, and therefore had a great deal of say in the guest list. Often many of the guests were distant relatives or friends of the bride's parents whom the couple had never met.

Things have changed recently, and weddings are seen less often seen as an opportunity to get Great Aunt Thelma out of the cupboard. So, try to understand your daughter's point of view if she would rather invite her friends and closer relatives.

How to keep the peace

Worried that relatives may be offended if they are not invited?

Option one, generally ill-advised, is to demand they be included.

Option two is to take some of the burden off your daughter by phoning the relatives, explaining that numbers are limited and arranging to visit them afterwards with the video, or send them copies of the photos.

Guest list dilemma

If you are not hosting the wedding, you may not have a great deal of say in the guest list. If you are hosting and can't agree on the guest list together, a good solution is a three-way split: one third for your guests, one third for the bride's and one third for the groom's.

No kids allowed!

Many venues nowadays are not suitable for
children, either in size or facilities, and your
daughter may decide she wants a child-free
wedding. This is often a difficult decision, so
offer to phone relatives with children to
explain the situation.

A dad, not just a wallet

A DAD, NOT JUST A WALLET

While money is very rarely an
unacceptable offering, there are
other ways to make sure your
daughter has the day of
her dreams.

A helping hand

Many brides take on too much of
the wedding planning. Why not make
sure your daughter knows she can
delegate a few tasks to you?

Or try a few of these suggestions…

Home, Dad!

If you're one of those dads who spent
a whole decade as an unpaid chauffeur,
ferrying your daughter between ballet
lessons, netball practice and sleepovers,
then you know what's coming next.
Can you offer to pick up chair covers,
drop off cake samples or even drive
her to her dress fitting?

All in a good cause

If you have a particular skill, don't be shy in coming forward.

Do you know about wine? Offer to taste the wine she is thinking of having at her reception.

Know a little about photography? Perhaps you could help review the work of potential snappers.

A DAD, NOT JUST A WALLET

Make her an offer she can't refuse...
Can you help by offering your garden as
a convenient location for a marquee?
Maybe you could lend your cherished
sports car to the best man to make sure
the groom arrives at the ceremony in style?
Or perhaps you're happy to help address
those 120 envelopes for the invitations.

The interest rate

Nothing is guaranteed to upset a bride more than her parents appearing uninterested in her wedding planning. Offer to go and see the venue after she's chosen it; keep up to date with the ins and outs of ordering the dress. Little gestures such as these are worth their weight in gold!

A DAD, NOT JUST A WALLET

A friend in need...

Sometimes your daughter might need a
shoulder to cry on, or someone on whom
to vent her frustration at not being able to
find a convertible Robin Reliant to get her
to the church. Or perhaps she's simply
had too much advice from well-meaning
mothers, bridesmaids, sisters and friends.
Let her know she can rely on you to
offer a sympathetic ear!

Don't feel left out

If you're not walking your little princess to the altar, don't worry. If you've got this far in the book, you'll know already that this is far from the only way you can play a part in your daughter's wedding. She knows this too, so why not put your heads together and plan a role just for you?

Which dad should make the speech?
The bride wants to include both her father and her stepfather in the speeches – but who makes the father of the bride speech?

One bride solved this dilemma extremely effectively by asking her stepfather to compere all the speeches, introducing each speaker and explaining their relationship to the bride and groom. Her father gave the father of the bride speech. One bride, two speakers, both able to contribute to her special day.

Top table dilemma

The bride wants her father and stepfather
on the top table, but worries that her dad
is afraid people will think this is weird.

As more couples have divorced parents,
wedding traditions are changing. Don't
worry about what used to be the 'correct'
way of doing things. If it makes your
daughter happy, it's probably the right
thing to do! If you're unhappy, talk to your
daughter rationally about her decisions.
But be prepared to back down eventually!

Sister act

Some lucky families seem to be blessed with sisters who are the best of friends. However, if the relationship is not so perfect, be prepared for the planning period to show the cracks. If the relationship erupts, be on hand to lend an ear, but stay impartial. Taking sides is never a good idea!

Sibling rivalry

Some brides are put under pressure from
their parents to choose their nieces or
nephews as bridesmaids or page boys.

If you're blessed with angelic grandchildren,
then, of course, you'd love to see them play
a part in your daughter's special day. But
if she's not keen, don't push it. After all, if
they're that cute, they'll surely be
snapped up by another bride!

Up-to-date dads

UP-TO-DATE DADS

If you got married a while ago,
then you may find that traditions have
changed considerably over the past
decade or so.

Wedding etiquette has caught up with
the fact that times are changing…

Gift list etiquette

As recently as five years ago, it was
considered very bad manners to enclose
your gift list with your invitations.
Nowadays, it's considered more polite to
send the list direct to guests, so saving
them the inconvenience of requesting it
from the bride's mother or other holder.

Money

Asking for money also used to be a no-no. However, many couples would now like to receive one big gift, such as a new sofa or bathroom, rather than knives and forks, which they may already have.

Set up an account

If your daughter wants to do this, suggest she sets up a separate account and lets people know that they can send money direct to you to put in the account. This way, guests feel assured that the couple will receive a great gift of money to spend on something they'll really enjoy.

Room at the top

If your daughter decides to break away from tradition and dispense with the top table, or even a cake, she is not alone. In large and complex families, organizing the top table may just become too political, and it's often easier to simply do without.

Times have changed

Couples no longer feel obliged to
stick to traditions they don't want.
Take the bride who replaced the
cake with a pile of doughnuts topped
by a Homer Simpson doll. The couple
loved it – and so did the guests!

World wide weddings

If you're helping the bride find the perfect pink convertible Beetle or napkins in the precise shade of baby blue, your first stop should be the Internet.

At www. confetti.co.uk, for instance, you'll find advice, information and comprehensive lists of every photographer, master of ceremonies, marquee hirer, florist, dress shop, children's entertainer and more in the UK.

World wide weddings

The bride might be looking for the perfect poem to read, or the sheet music for a song she wants a friend to sing at the ceremony. Go online to get your research done in double-quick time, from the comfort of your own chair!

World wide weddings

Why not surprise her by creating a wedding
website for her? She'll love it, and even a
novice can build a professional-looking (and
free!) site using the Confetti web pages.

What to wear

WHAT TO WEAR

The bride usually has a strong preference as to whether the men in the wedding party should wear morning dress or lounge suits. You should expect to be consulted, but if your views differ wildly from those of your daughter, you might have to yield gracefully. Basically, if the groom is wearing morning dress, you should, too.

Coordination

Unless you already have a suit of your own, consult with the groom about hiring similar outfits so that you achieve a coordinated effect on the day. The groom, best man, ushers, bride's father and groom's father should all look similar.

Remember that a hired suit needs to be fitted and ordered well in advance so that it is ready for the big day. Of course, as father of the bride you can wear ceremonial attire, such as a kilt or dress uniform, if you are entitled to do so.

Personalize your outfit

Even when you're dressed like the other guys, you'll still want to look a little different, but do this by means of a different-coloured waistcoat, special buttonhole or fancy cravat. Don't spring any wild colour or pattern surprises on your daughter!

Top tips for looking good

1 For heaven's sake, get measured properly – especially if you suspect your waist measurement may have expanded. Admitting you're no longer a size 34 could save you from having to spend your wedding day holding your breath in case you pop a button.

Top tips for looking good
2 Accessorize!
Think smart cufflinks, shirt studs,
a decent watch (not the one you got
free at the garage), a tie pin, bow tie,
buttonhole, braces, a cummerbund,
waistcoat, handkerchief – and, of
course, your shoes, which really
need to be in keeping with the
whole get-up.

Top tips for looking good

3 So well groomed you're often mistaken for Roger Moore? Or do people have difficulty telling you and Bob Geldof apart? Either way, this really is a day for looking your best. And that means a haircut, a good shave and even a manicure. Go on, you might enjoy it!

Top tips for looking good

4 Check your outfit two weeks before in case you've lost weight, collected the wrong size shirt or there's been a bad attack of moths!

5 Wedding photographs are a long-lasting souvenir of the big day. Just remember the best tip: don't slouch.

How to tie ties

The following are simple instructions for
the four classic tie styles.

The Bow Tie

1

2

3

4

5

6

The Bow Tie

The Bow Tie should be tied as follows:

1 Start with A 4cm (1½in) below B.
2 Take A over, then under, B.
3 Double B in half and place across the collar points.
4 Hold B with thumb and index finger; drop A over.
5 Pull A through a little, then double A and pass behind, then through the hole in front.
6 Poke resulting loop through; even it out, then tighten.

THE FATHER OF THE BRIDE'S WEDDING

The Four in Hand

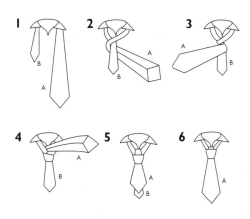

The Four in Hand

The Four in Hand should be tied as follows:

1 Start with A about 50cm (20in) below B.
2 Take A behind B.
3 Continue wrapping right round.
4 Pull A up through the loop.
5 Pull A down through loop in front.
6 Tighten.

The Windsor

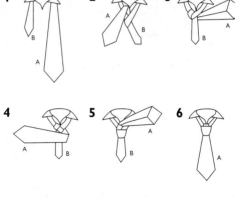

The Windsor

The Windsor should be tied as follows:

1 Start with A about 60cm (24in) below B.
2 Take A behind B and up through loop.
3 Bring A over and behind B.
4 Take A down through loop again.
5 Then over and up through loop.
6 Bring through the knot and tighten.

The Half Windsor

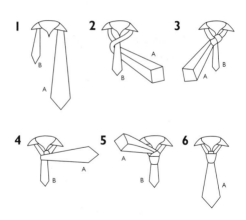

The Half Windsor

A Half Windsor is a kind of reverse Windsor.

1 Start in the same position as the Windsor.
2 Loop A behind B.
3 Bring A up into the loop and out behind
B on the other side.
4 Fold A back across B.
5 Tuck A up through the loop.
6 Bring A back through the knot and tighten.

The big day

THE BIG DAY

The wedding rehearsal will normally take
place during the week before the wedding
day, or even the day before.
All the bridal party, including the bride,
groom, best man and chief bridesmaid,
attend the rehearsal, possibly accompanied
by the mother and father of the bride and
groom. The minister will run through the
service, everyone will be shown where to
stand before and during the service, and
the rough timings of the service will
be finalized.

The wedding rehearsal

As well as being a practice run for the service, the rehearsal also serves to bring together any members of the wedding party who have not yet met. The bride and groom often take the opportunity to host a dinner for the wedding party as a token of their appreciation.

THE BIG DAY

Morning has broken

This is going to be one of the most hectic days of your life, so make sure you've organized and double-checked everything the night before. Go over the final version of your speech, and give a copy to your wife or another relative in case of disaster!

Things to do

Call the car in advance to check there are
no hold-ups. Reassure your daughter you've
done this, then see to your own nerves
with a (small) glass of champagne.

THE BIG DAY

Get me to the church on time!
Your most important task is to support
your daughter, calm her nerves and, above
all, get her to the church or register
office on time!

You will also need to make sure the cars
arrive as arranged to take the bridesmaids,
mother of the bride and other members
of the family to the ceremony.

Your words of wisdom

When helping your daughter into the bridal car, make sure that her fabulous dress is not crushed. This will probably be the only time you have together today, so if you want to say anything to her, now's the time. Most brides are very nervous at this point, so a few words of support will be appreciated. Make sure you've got a few tissues in case her feelings get the better of her!

THE BIG DAY

Who gives this woman in marriage?
If the marriage is taking place in church, a
hymn is usually sung once you have walked
your daughter up the aisle. The vicar then
states the reason for the gathering and asks
if anyone knows of any reason why the
marriage should not take place.
Having received the couple's agreement to
be married, the vicar asks who is giving the
bride away. The bride hands her bouquet
to the chief bridesmaid and you place
your daughter's right hand in that of the
vicar, who gives it to the groom.

Civil ceremonies

If the marriage is taking place at a register office, it is up to your daughter to decide whether she wants to enter accompanied by you or perhaps her chief attendant, because there is no established etiquette involved. As her father, however, you are the usual choice.

Where should you sit?

Traditionally, during the ceremony you and
the bride's mother sit together in the front
row on the left-hand side.

The procession

In most church weddings, once the couple are officially husband and wife, you escort the groom's mother to the vestry for the signing of the register. At the end of the ceremony, you follow the bride's mother and the groom's father down the aisle, escorting the groom's mother on your right-hand side.

To the reception!

Sometimes the wedding ceremony will take place in the same location as the reception. If this is not the case, expect some photos to be taken before you leave for the reception. Obviously you don't ride with your daughter to the reception, but take your place, usually in the third car, following the bridesmaids and best man, or in the fourth car, accompanying the groom's mother.

THE FATHER OF THE BRIDE'S WEDDING

All line up!

Traditionally, the father and mother of the bride are the hosts. If you are to welcome guests in a formal receiving line, your place is second in the line, after the bride's mother.

Your responsiblities

If the bride and groom prefer to welcome
everyone on their own, your job is to
circulate among the guests, and
make introductions. Usually you are
responsible for the free flow of drink,
and, for all the obvious reasons, you
will probably want to keep an eye
on what's being consumed.

The speech

Speeches usually take place after the meal
has finished and before the cutting of the
cake. As the first person to speak, you
should welcome the guests, say how
pleased you are to have the groom as
your son-in-law, and congratulate the
happy couple. Then you – or your
chosen substitute – can make your
speech, finishing up with a toast
to the bride and groom. Once that's
over, you can relax.

Host duties

You might, nevertheless, want to keep an eye out for any elderly relatives who look as though they might be flagging (or any younger ones who are looking a bit 'tired and emotional')! Enlist the help of the ushers to perform your duties as host.

The father of the bride is the first to speak, and so your speech is a kind of scene-setter. It's generally expected to be the least funny and most sentimental, which for some is a blessing and others a challenge!

What to say

Your speech is also made on behalf of the
bride's mother, unless she is also going to
make a speech. If she has passed away,
then this may be the moment to say a
few words in her memory.

Traditional contents

Traditionally, you speak first and:

- Thank the guests for coming to the wedding and attending such a special day.
- Remember to mention anyone who has travelled especially far.
- Thank anyone involved in planning (and paying for) the wedding.
- Tell your daughter how proud you are of her...

Traditional contents

- Welcome your new son-in-law into your family.
- Reminisce about your daughter's pre-wedding years.
- Wish the newlyweds success and happiness in the future.
- Propose a toast to the bride and groom.

Alternative contents

You could also:

- Make a joint speech with your wife.
- Share the stage with a godfather or stepfather.
- Simply thank everyone for coming and propose a toast.
- Show a short film or candid camera shots of your daughter as a child!

First things first

If you feel that making a speech will be a bit of an ordeal, concentrate on the reason why you're making it in the first place. Bearing this in mind will help you make your speech personal, interesting, endearing and often funny!

The rules – think ahead
Don't leave your speech till the last minute.
Whatever time frame you have, give it your
undivided attention.

The rules – keep it short

Brevity truly is the soul of wit. Some speakers plan optional sections that can be cut if the speech isn't doing too well. At any rate, you should time your speech and stick to it – five minutes is perfectly long enough.

The rules – include everyone

Make sure your speech is accessible to everyone present. Many people will know only half of the wedding party (if that), and they may not even know you. In-jokes and favourite anecdotes should be told in such a way that everyone can enjoy them – so explain any un-obvious references as you go.

The rules – do your homework

Make yourself sit down and write out your ideas. This process will help spark other ideas.

The rules – practice makes perfect

Reading your speech out again and
again – preferably to other people – is
essential when practising. Listening to a
recording of yourself can be useful, too.
Listen out for any sections where
you speak too fast, or where the
point you're making is unclear,
and revise accordingly.

The rules – get it in writing

You may have practised your speech so hard that you're sure you know it by heart. Keep your text handy anyway – the stress of speaking can sometimes cause people to forget their lines.

Coping with nerves

Relax. It's your time, so take it. Everyone will listen to what you have to say because they want to. The speeches are always fun. Remember this and you'll deliver your speech with confidence and ease.

Coping with nerves

Resist the temptation to drown your nerves with drink. Allow yourself one drink but make that the limit. Have a drink as a reward afterwards. For now, keeping a clear head will see you at your best.

Don't sweat it!
If you're just not cut out for public
speaking, don't be afraid to co-opt a
stand in. They'll be honoured.

Alternatively, here are a few short
examples of speeches you might like
to read out...

Thanking people – samples

Laura and Garry have worked very hard to organize and pay for today, and it's been worth it. This is a lovely reception and everything looks perfect. I'm proud of the pair of you!

Thanking people – samples

I would like to say a special thank you today to John's mother, who has been an unflappable oasis of calm and rationality during such disasters as the napkins being slightly the wrong shade of pink, or the bride's shoes arriving only three months ahead of the big day. We couldn't have organized this – or paid for it! – without her, so thank you.

Thanking people – samples

I must say I'm surprised it's raining today.
Justine's mother and aunt Sally have been
such terrific wedding organizers that
I assumed they could also control
the weather!

Praising your daughter – samples

The house has seemed very quiet since Lucy left home. You can barely hear anything but the sound of my wallet sighing with relief.

Praising your daughter – samples

Nicola has had many roles in life, all of which she has shone in. She has been a student, a sister, a banker, a friend, a daughter, but never has she been more radiant than she is today, as a bride.

Praising your daughter – samples

Emily was always a tomboy. I think her first words were 'Manchester United'. As a child she was never happier than when she was climbing a tree or heading a ball. I can hardly believe that the vision of loveliness before me today is my daughter. You'll never manage a decent goal kick in that frock though, love.

THE FATHER OF THE BRIDE'S WEDDING

Welcoming the groom – samples

The groom's father has been sharing a few stories with me about Phil's teenage years. All I can say is, it's with a mixture of fascination and horror that I say, 'Welcome to the family, Phil!'

Welcoming the groom – samples

I'd like to take a moment to welcome Sean to the family. I've heard that he was a precocious child. He walked and talked before he was one; he could read and write by the time he was four, and could forge his parents' signatures by the time he was eight! Now he has Fiona to keep him on the straight and narrow, and we'll be watching his progress with interest!

Welcoming the groom – samples

Melanie always claimed that she would never meet the right man. Well, I'm pleased to say that she has been proved completely wrong. She has found the perfect partner in John, and I am delighted he has become a part of the family.

Thanking the guests – samples

Thank you all for coming and sharing this special day with Nicola and John. It's quite a journey for some of you, and I'm delighted to know that so many of you consider this lovely couple worth it.

Thanking the guests – samples

It's wonderful to see so many people who've travelled so far to join us in our celebrations today. Sadly, Bob and Alice were unable to get over from Australia, and they are sorely missed today. But I know that they're thinking about us, and raising a glass to Kate and Sam, even as we speak. Or they will be when they wake up!

'To the happy couple!'

For richer, for poorer, in sickness and in health...pray charge your glasses and toast our delightful newlyweds, Jane and John!

To the happy couple!'
*Ladies and gentlemen, boys and girls…
Please be upstanding and raise your
glasses to… the wonderful couple!*

'To the happy couple!'

Please join me in wishing our bride and groom health, wealth, friendship and a long and fulfilling life. To Sandra and Gareth!

Final words of wisdom

This is an important day in your daughter's life and in the history of your family – but it's not worth falling out over. Always try to keep the peace and trust your daughter's decisions.

Final words of wisdom

Goethe said, 'The sum which two married people owe to one another defies calculation. It is an infinite debt, which can only be discharged through all eternity.'

This should not apply to your bank account after you've finished paying for the party.

ABOUT CONFETTI.CO.UK

Confetti.co.uk is the UK's leading wedding and special occasion website, helping more than 400,000 brides, grooms and guests every month.
To find out more or to order your confetti party brochure or wedding and party stationery brochure,
visit: www.confetti.co.uk
email: info@confetti.co.uk
call: 0870 840 6060
visit Confetti at: 80 Tottenham Court Road, London or at The Light, Leeds LS1 8TL

Other books in this series include: *Your Daughter's Wedding, How to Write a Wedding Speech, Men at Weddings, The Bride's Wedding* and *The Groom's Wedding*